EASY HOW-TO GROW TREES FOR PRIVACY SCREENS AND WINDBREAKS -

10 Fast Growing Trees You Should Plant

WHAT ABOUT PLANTING SCREENS AND WINDBREAKS?

One of the most sought after desires or goals in the home land-scape design, is privacy. Green screens, privacy fences, and the like have become very popular over the last number of years. How to achieve it, at a minimal cost, and in the shortest time possible, are key questions asked. Building a fence or wall can work, at least to some extent. They can be quickly built, but the costs can be prohibitive, and there may be a limitation as to the effect-ive height. The living fence can be that alternative. Planting trees for windbreaks and screens is actually easy, and there are some suggestions as to which trees to use.

In this guide, we firstly talk about Screens, the basics. Then, we talk about trees and notes on several that we think are more applicable and reasonably available. The last section is some of the how-to information most useful for any tree or shrub-plant-ing project, whether for screens, commercial uses, or for the home and garden landscape.

Whichever it is called, a Privacy Screen, Living Fence, Green Barrier, Live Barrier, Windbreak, Shelterbelt, or other terms, planting trees and or shrubs are very popularly used as fences and walls. For the most part, these terms will be used interchangeably. There are as many species of trees in which to plant, as there are variables that will effect where you plant such screens. Which trees to plant, evergreens or broad leaf types, as well as climate considerations, soil conditions, watering, planting techniques, and other factors often short-circuit the project because it seems so complex. These don't have to be complex questions or concerns, as these factors can be simply explained, and will help push a planting project forward.

In the landscape design, two goals often stand out - fast growth and evergreen. Although worthwhile and desirable, the two are often not attainable without some give and take. That is to say, there are some great fast-growers, but they are typically broadleaf trees that drop their leaves in the fall. The fast growing evergreens, don't grow nearly as fast as the broadleafs (or broad leafs), but once they reach the desired size, they are green year-round. Therefore, plant both - the faster growing broadleafs such as the Ameri-Willow hybrid, poplars, and others, as well as plant some of the faster growing evergreens. The one gives you the instant screening you want, while buying you time for the evergreens to grow to size. Think about it.

Often people want to know "how fast" they will grow, and "how far apart" to plant them. The growth rate really is a complex set of inter-acting factors that are unique to each specific area and type of tree, but generally an average rate is commonly used, with the idea of showing relative growth for comparisons.

The willows and poplars typically grow the fastest, up to 8 feet or more a year, but there are other trees that grow anywhere from four to ten feet a year. There are so many great and wonderful trees that can work well for screens and windbreaks, but there are ten that seem to stand out as good candidates. These ten have the broadest reach across the country, under most growing conditions. Not an exclusive bunch, by no means, but consider these as a "starter kit" into a broader world. These are good solid selections for many screen and windbreak applications.

There are many trees to chose from, certainly each has its own merits. We came up with "our" list of ten trees, that "we" like and think will do well in most growing conditions, over the greater part of the country. This group, the "Ten", includes the Ameri-Willow hybrid, Hybrid Poplar, Quaking Aspen, European White Birch, Red Mulberry, Ohio Buckeye, Red Maple, Scotch Pine, Douglas-Fir, and Norway Spruce. To add a few alternate trees, we might add the White Willow, Horse Chestnut, Northern Catalpa, Ponderosa Pine, White Spruce, and even the Colorado Blue Spruce. These are all unique and different, hardy, and can be planted across much of the country, under most growing conditions. More in depth explanation below.

DESIGNING AND PLANTING GREEN BARRIERS

There is a difference between privacy screens and other barriers. A windbreak is an effective barrier, several rows wide, and should be composed of several types of trees and tall shrubs. This is different than a fence line border, or privacy screen, which are basically planting trees in one or two rows.

Depending on the project and the space available, additional rows might be added. Each additional row is planted offset or zigzagged to the others. The more rows you can plant, the greater the barrier will become. This is particularly true for windbreaks and noise barriers.

SHELTERBELTS WERE THE FIRST WINDBREAKS AND PRIVACY SCREENS

The big surge of shelterbelt plantings in the mid-western states was during the Dust-Bowl years of the 1930's. That is where this idea of planting several rows of trees and shrubs to create a barrier against the weather became popular. On and off through the years following the various wars and international conflicts, the shelterbelts were still being planted nationwide. The ecological revolution embraced the tree planting concept, as did the energy saving era that followed. It just made good cents! For wildlife enhancement, the oasis created by the linear islands, helped to boost sagging habitats.

The rage these days is to plant privacy screens and shelterbelts to block out the neighbor's junkyard, or disguise those sprouting sub-divisions. Interesting to note, that despite the era or the terminology, the idea of tree planting in blocks remains popular. Why? Simply because it works.

There is no more simple way to manipulate the local environment, than to plant trees. Whether it feeds that desire to control our surroundings, or heightens some spiritual sense, mass tree planting is really the cheapest and most practical means to achieve a number of land use goals.

Cost is always a consideration, whether buying a few trees to screen off the neighbors, or when developing reforestation and afforestation projects. We can't escape that. More than just a dollar for dollar return on the cash outlays, a well designed screen or barrier offers more in tangible and intangible goods. plant trees. Whether it feeds that desire to control our surroundings, or heightens some spiritual sense, mass tree planting is really the cheapest and most practical means to achieve a number of land use goals.

Perhaps the primary purpose is protection from the weather, which includes protecting the soil from erosion, and cutting heating costs to the home and summer cooling expense. Also, holding back the drifting snows, or the slow release of water to the creeks and channels, renewed habitat for dwindling populations of critters, all are difficult to assign a dollar value onto. Collecting nuts and berries from wisely planted barriers is entertaining and feeds local wildlife. Planting trees and shrubs that can offer products like firewood, or materials to make baskets or other crafts, along with selling a sawlog or two, are long-term things that do relate to that dollar investment. Of course, talking about money, the value of land with a massive shelterbelt is far greater than bare lifeless dirt.

The greatest of our renewable resources are the trees we plant, whether as dust-bowl plantings or for privacy, the idea of planting trees as barriers remain popular.

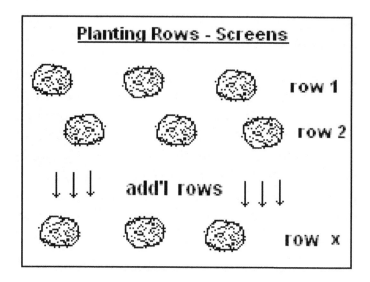

Green Screens - the "How-to"

Ok, for more substance and less philosophy, here's a more technical version. The idea of screens is protection from the weather, privacy, and there are the side benefits of: wildlife enhancement, aesthetics, forest resources, and others. The same techniques and process are applicable to all shelterbelts and green barriers, whatever the desired purpose.

How large and developed a planting, depends on the space available and the budget. The larger the area to plant, the greater the options in the design. The surrounding properties and topography can also shape your design. And of course nothing is cheap, in both time and cash expenses, but as an investment, tree planting offers more than a dollar for dollar return. The idea of the shelterbelt is a series of rows, planted either surrounding the property, or just in the direction of the prevailing wind or storms. The rows can all be the same trees, one massive block, but the idea of mixing makes a lot of sense. Different trees and shrubs offer the best long term plan because insect and diseases come and go, hit one species of trees, or maybe a few, but the rest of the block is less likely to be susceptible. Once planted, the trees usually don't get any care, watering being the most critical, so selection of plants to use is worthwhile.

Mix and match, fast growing trees, slower growing trees, conifers, tall and short shrubs, each in their own row, or mixed within the same row. Trees are generally planted ten feet apart, and shrubs can be planted four feet apart. This is a good general rule, and can certainly be changed. From these general spacing rules, measure your property and do some simple calculations. How many rows do you want, or how many do you have room for? And if planted say ten feet apart, you can come up with a quantity of trees needed.

The thicker the block, the more shelter it will provide. Plant the tallest trees in the center rows, and the shorter trees on the out-side facing the oncoming storms, the wind-ward side. Outside of that, plant tall and short shrub rows. On the inside of the block, you can mirror the other side or just plant for eye appeal, like a row of flowering or fruit-bearing shrubs, or smaller trees. Plant fast growing trees to add some early protection, and then the slower growing trees and shrubs will fill in later. The reasoning is that you want some screening right away, and then over the fol-lowing years, the stronger and longer lived plants will take over.

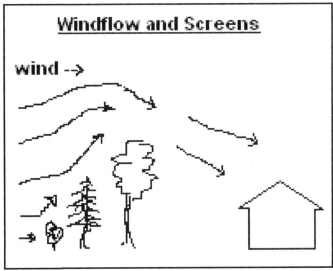

The effect you want is large-scale aerodynamics, like a ramp to scoop the oncoming winds up and then over the block. There is a relationship between shelterbelt height and length of calmness on the lee-side, or inside of the block where the house or buildings are. It's something like one foot of shelterbelt height will produce protection for one and a half to two feet of distance inside the block. So for a block that has trees fifty feet tall, there should be much calmer weather 75 to 100 feet inside.

Then select the trees and plants that are suited to your climate. If the planned shelterbelt is to be in a dry climate, plan on some type of irrigation system to at least get the plants established. There is some early maintenance that will help, like weed control until the trees are taller, and then a shot of fertilizer to start the second year will help with establishment. Outside of that, there is little work that needs to be done. Watering, weeding, and fertilizing, and the rest is watching.

The most popular fast growing trees are the hybrid willows and poplars, and the oaks, maples, ash, and other hardwoods are good slower growing trees. The pines are conifers would be considered in the slower growing trees group. The other conifers are generally slower growing than the pines, the firs, cedars, and spruces, but all can be planted as well. It makes sense to plant trees that bear edibles like walnuts and mulberries, and regular fruit trees can be incorporated into the row system pretty easily. The same with the shrub rows, cranberries and blueberries, or hazelnuts and Prunus species, can add a great food source for wildlife and people.

Every green barrier design is different, and depends on the designer's taste and space available. There are many ideas to incorporate: rows, blocks, edibles, aesthetics, heights, growth rates, and long term benefits, all which make the planning challenging, but worthwhile.

MINI-SCREEN PLANTINGS

Having a screen or green fence of some type, sounds appealing, but space may be limited. There is a formula used in some books in planning windscreens, like a foot of plant height equates to wind protection of a foot and a half of the leeward side, that can help with your planning.

That's fine, but in reality, it comes down to time and space. You have X amount of space between your property lines, with a building(s) in the middle, and you want protection now. Its pretty simple. Not everyone has room for a massive shelterbelt, so it really comes down to planning your landscape design to incorporate many of the same elements. Pen and paper, and some measurements works well.

You can have a mini-shelterbelt with relatively simple planting. For many areas, storms follow a pattern or track, such as coming in from the southwest and moving northeast. If the bulk of your storms, especially the wind storms, follows a pattern like that, then its easy to know where to place your plants -- so they block the wind. That's perpendicular to the prevailing wind or storms. This is where you want the tallest and thickest plantings, but of course you have to consider existing trees, streets, driveways, etc. The difference between windscreens and shelterbelts is the mass. The more room available, the more rows you can plant, and the more effective the barrier will be.

In a limited space, it comes down to adding a line trees, or maybe just adding a few tall shrubs to fill in the holes.

Because many of the trees and shrubs will lose their leaves, you want to include conifers or at least plant more rows. Bare trunks do add some protection. In an ideal shelterbelt, you have a row of fast growing trees like poplars or willows in the middle, then on either side, have a row of conifers. Then in rows outside of the conifers, you have rows of tall shrubs, and maybe short shrubs beyond that. There can be any number of rows, again dependent on space, but 3 to 5 rows is common.

The growth pattern is like a triangle, with the fast growing trees in the center, and the slower and smaller plants on the outside. The poplars and willows give the fastest protection, then a number of years later, the conifers get tall enough to make the wall stronger. The shrub rows on the outside adds "scoop" to the winds to help push them over the wall. In the mini-barrier, the rows might be fewer and the planting can be closer. It's better to plant closer than too wide, since its easier to cut out trees than to add new ones.

So looking at your yard, can you add a row or several rows? Draw it out on paper planning 6-10 feet between trees, and 3-4 feet between shrubs. With existing trees or other obstructions, maybe just fill in with shrubs or small trees. For open areas, plan the row idea. If you have ten feet of space, you can have two or three rows, so it doesn't require a great deal of space. When adding shrubs, eye appeal is important. Landscaping is all about eye appeal, even when planting barriers.

Look at planting as a triangle or stair-step, with the smaller and more colorful plants leading up to the taller layers.

EVERGREEN SCREENS

Fast growing hardwoods (or broadleafs) are fine to use, but they drop their leaves in the Fall. The question then comes about, can evergreens (or conifers) work instead? Which evergreen trees can be used to block out the neighbors' junk yard, make a barrier to calm down the highway noise, and create a green wall from the lookie-loos? Any tree will be an improvement, but some are better, which depends on a number of factors.

Using conifers as screens is great because they are solid year-round, versus the fast-growing hardwoods that drop their laves in the fall. The trade off is that the conifers generally grow much slower than the hardwoods. Still, depending on the site conditions and long-term plan, conifers offer a lot of possibilities.

Selecting the conifers to use depends partly on the Plant Zones. Zone 6 and above is basically the middle of the country and south. The cypress and cypress-like species are less cold tolerant than the needle-bearing pine-like trees. For Plant Zone 6 and above, then the Arizona Cypress is about the fastest growing. Zones 5 are the lower limits to the Cedars - Port Orford, Incense, and Western Red. Arbor Vitae will go down below Zone 5 to Zone 4, and maybe into Zone 3.

The Redwoods vary considerably depending on the species. The Coast one is for Zone 7 and above, the Dawn will go down to 4, and the Giant Sequoia is considered a Zone 5. The true firs and Douglas-Fir will go down to Zones 3 to 5, the pines are 2-5, and the spruces are good down to Zones 2 to 5.

Each of these grow at different rates, but in general the cypress-like trees will grow faster than the needle-like trees. Growth can be somewhat increased by weed control, watering, and fertilizing, and increasing the amount of light available (as with trimming the surrounding trees).

Now, shade is another consideration for conifer screens. The pines especially prefer the full sun, but most trees do anyways. Arbor Vitae does ok with shade, but the growth rate slows, as will any tree. Western Red Cedar can grow great in very heavy shade, as will the true firs and spruces, but shade means slower than normal growth.

For wet areas, plant Western Red Cedar, or Coast Redwood if the Zone is 7+, but generally not the pines, which like it drier. The other conifers are mixed in between.

For drier conditions, the Arizona Cypress is the best, then the pines. Adding a mulch layer around the tree is a cheap and easy way to conserve moisture and moderate the soil temperatures for the roots, along with keeping control over the weeds.

What mess? The nice part about planting the conifers is that there is very little to clean up, versus
the hardwoods. They will lose needles and such, but not like the quantity from a leafy tree, like a maple or oak.

Here is an important factor, tree selection for your area. Understandably you want it now, but save yourself the headaches, expense, and future hassles by selecting the right trees for the project. Cost is always a factor, not just buying big trees versus small ones, but also planting, watering, time, and upkeep costs too. The other thing to consider is the outcome. What will you achieve, and what value have you added to your property. Is the goal a screen to block out the view of the neighbors, reduce wind, noise abatement, visuals, or other objectives? Knowing the project, you can better design the barrier. Trees and plants for the home, farm, or commercial project, are an investment.

Fence lines or border trees, which also work as solid screens, are the Ameri-Willow, Lombardy Poplar, other fast-growing broad-leafs, and most of the conifers. Plant one row, and the spacing can vary depending on how much you want to block the view. The willows and poplars will grow really fast, but drop their leaves in the fall. The conifers will stay thick and green year-round, but are much slower growing. The birch and aspens have fall coloration, and the flowering cherries, pears, and plums add a nice visual effect in the springtime. Here again, the fence line planting depends on the goal or desired look.

If space is more available to let the trees spread out, then the Leyland Cypress and Hybrid Poplar, and others make effective screens. Plant one or more rows. These grow fast, and the cypress stays green, while the poplar drops its leaves in the fall. By planting a row of fast-growing hardwoods, and a row of slower-growing evergreens, you can have year-round screening, and fast growth!

For privacy screens, one or more rows can be planted. Ideally, it would be nice to have super-fast growing evergreens, and only need to plant a single row. Unfortunately, most of the evergreens grow fairly slow. Some like the Cherry Laurel, Leyland Cypress, Mondell Pine, to name some of the more popular types, can grow fairly fast. Still, the broadleafs, namely the willows and poplars, grow much faster, and can produce a modest screen within a couple years. Climate or Plant Zones, and growing conditions will influence the species that can grow best in a particular area.

Some of the faster growers like the willows and poplars like wetter ground, and can handle ponded water for extended periods of time, whereas many of the evergreens like the pines prefer drier soils and non-ponded conditions. But often you want to plant the different types of trees together. The trick is to prepare the ground before you plant. Make low spots (or a trench with a tractor) for the trees that like moister conditions, and mounds to plant the trees that prefer drier conditions. It adds to the work, but it can make all the difference.

For thick, year round screens, evergreens, like the pines, firs, spruces, and cedars do well. Douglas-Fir can grow fairly fast, about 1 to 3 feet a year, but the others will grow about 1 foot a year. Here is that time factor, but the outcome is impressive. Starting with larger trees will trim off a couple years, but the costs will be higher. But if a row of faster-growing broadleafs is also planted, you would get a fast screen, while the evergreens are slowly growing. Then once the evergreens reach the desired size, the broadleafs can be cut down if desired.

A screen around a pool might be planted with tall shrubs like the Aronia, Hazelnut, Dogwoods, Red-Tip Photinia, and others, instead of trees. The roots systems will stay fairly small and not interfere with the pool, and they won't shade the water. For key spots, such as to block a neighbor's window, plant one or more trees, but further away from the pool. Planting three trees (the same species, or a mix) in a triangle planting pattern can make for a very effective block.

For value and beauty, lines of birch or aspen along the driveway or a fence, really are spectacular. They don't make thick effect-ive screens by themselves, but for increasing value to a property, how can you beat a line with those? Colorado Blue Spruce is also a choice for "valuable" lines. Here again, consider combining the hardwoods and evergreens for a year-round green barrier.

There are other trees and tall shrubs that can be used in lines, like buckeyes, maples, pines, and more, but the project depends on your needs and desired outcome. Think about it.

Spacing, is a factor of available space and the trees' normal shape. The general rule of thumb is 6 to 10 feet apart. Slower growing and narrower shaped trees can be planted closer together so a line or screen will fill in sooner. For faster growing or wider-shaped types, then planting can be spaced wider. Planting two staggered or offset rows can change the spacing also. Instead of planting a poplar (for example) six feet apart, two offset rows can be planted at eight or ten feet apart. The effective spacing is then four or five feet apart. This creates a denser barrier that grows in faster. It helps to draw your plans on paper and try different arrangements and types of trees and shrubs.

Planting is easy, but planting a long row or several rows can make for a long day! Dig a hole a little bit larger than the roots are wide (when spread out). Place the tree in the hole so the roots can then be covered completely. Scoop the soil back into the hole. Water it, and that's basically it! You can mix in organic materials or bagged soil mixes, but this is not needed unless your soil is heavy clay, rocky, or very sandy. Do place a layer of mulch around the trees to help conserve water, suppress weeds, and help insulate roots from weather extremes.

Do not fertilize at the time of planting. Let the plants get settled in for a month or so before sprinkling a light fertilizer on the soil surface. Then when fertilizer is added, do water afterwards. This helps to rinse whatever might have gotten onto the plant leaves or stems, and then keeps it from washing away (as from storms). It also waters in the nitrogen, which can partly evaporate. Make sure the plants are watered well after fertilizing, also to reduce the chance of "burning" the feeder roots.

When to fertilize? Fertilize all trees and shrubs at least twice, in late winter or early spring, then again in late spring or early summer. Both fertilizations should be high in nitrogen, as that is the key nutrient, and that, which will have the greatest demand. During the growing season, when the tree leaves start to turn yellow, which is usually a sign of nitrogen deficiency, but use a well balanced type to assure the best results. If possible, a light or low-strength monthly fertilizing assures a steady supply of nutrients for the roots. The growth process demands a lot of nitrogen, singly the best nutrient, and any fertilizer can work fine. You might consider something like Miracle-Grow, Scotts, or Peter's, and even lawn fertilizer that is high in nitrogen. The added nitrogen will help the other soil nutrients become more available, and also hastens the breakdown of organic material. Fertilizer "packets", tablets, or stakes can work also.

A water basin around the trees can be helpful, but also not needed. The mulch layer will be effective in conserving water, but also plan on some type of watering system. Depending on the set-up, there are many ways to add water, a hose, sprinklers, a drip tube set-up, or even the bucket method. Remember, during the late spring through the summer months, water demand by the roots will greatly increase, so you may need to water more often or increase the volume for automated watering systems.

Lines of shrubs can create nice looking screens or barriers, blocking out the wind, unsightly neighbors, or just add an attractive boundary marking. The lowest cost and most beneficial form of fencing and green barriers is to plant trees, but first have a project goal in mind, and then choose the tree species to best fit your climate and growing conditions. There is a lot to consider, but its worth it.

RELATIVE GROWTH RATES

Now for screens and windbreaks, and any planting project, the question is which trees to use. Certainly, every tree species grows at a different rate, but there is and can be a considerable amount of growth variation within the same species. "How fast" does a tree grow? The answer is, "it depends".

Trees and plants are continually being hybridized, and new varieties seem to appear daily. Not that every new plant is better than the original, but overall, they have an improved performance in growth, disease resistance, or other desirable qualities.

For improving tree growth, it is worthwhile to start with quality trees.

Growth and growth rates are controlled by genetics, and in response to the environmental factors where that particular tree is planted. Here we're talking about genotypes and phenotypes. We have very little control over the genotype, the internal genetic character of trees, except for planting hybrids, but some control over the phenotype or external characters. In this respect, growth rate for a tree, is relative, relative to the site where its growing.

Yes, we'll compare some popular tree species, but having a brief course in Silviculture is worthwhile also.

Given a choice, a tree or any other plant would grow best and fastest in optimal conditions, where temperature, light, water, and nutrients is nearly perfect. We're talking about a greenhouse, where the growth rate can be maxed. In the real world, trees are subject to summer drought, early frosts, short growing seasons, etc., which are factors of our hands. What we can control are supplemental watering, weed control, fertilizing, and planting the right tree in the right spot, and planted the right way. Doing these things will affect the phenotype of the tree and growth can be improved.

Some trees grow better in shade than others, some like more water, but all plants prefer good soils with enough water and nutrients. Its also worth mentioning that if a tree is planted poorly, its growth rate will be reduced, which may not be evident for five or ten years. Ever plant a tree and it just sat there for years growing a few inches a time?

Given you can improve the water and fertilizer, etc. which trees grow how fast? Understand, this is a relative comparison. Growth rates will vary considerably based on your Plant Zone, and the conditions your trees are growing in.

The list of trees can be endless, but these are the ones we like. These are estimates, and your growth rates may vary depending on your specific growing conditions and climate. In general, you may see...

Broadleafs (Hardwoods) -

* Ameri-Willow - 8 to 15 ft./ yr, and possibly more!
* Weeping Willow - average 6 ft., can be 6-8 ft./yr.
* Willows (Other) - 4 to 8 ft./yr.
* Quaking Aspen - average 4 ft., can be 4-6 ft./yr.
* Black Cottonwood - average 6 ft., can be 6-10 ft./yr.
* Northern Cottonwood - average 6 ft. ,vary 6-10 ft./yr.
* Cottonless Cottonwood - average 6 ft., vary 6-10 ft./yr.
* Hybrid Poplar - average 8 ft., can be 8-12 ft./yr.
* Lombardy Poplar - average 6 ft., can be 8-10 ft./yr.
* Siouxland Poplar - average 8 ft., can be 8-10 ft./yr.
* Sweetgum - average 4 ft., can be 4-6ft./yr.
* American Sycamore - average 6 ft., can be 6-10 ft./yr.
* European White Birch - average 2 ft., can be 1-4 ft/yr.;
* Tree of Heaven- average 4 ft., can be 4-6 ft./yr.
* Paulownia - average 6 ft., can be 6-8 ft./yr.
* Siberian Elm - average 4 ft., can be 4-6 ft./yr.
* Sugar Maple - average 1.5 ft., can be 1-3 ft./yr.
* Red Maple - average 1.5 ft., can be 1-3 ft./yr.
* Red Oak - average 1 ft., can be 1-3 ft./yr.
* Hardwoods (General) - average 2 ft., can be 1-3 ft/yr.;

Conifers (Evergreens) -

* Leyland Cypress - 3 to 6 ft./yr.
* Coast Redwood - 2 to 8 ft./yr.
* Western Red Cedar - 1 to 3 ft./yr.
* Colorado Blue Spruce - average 1 ft.,vary 0.5-1.5 ft./yr.
* True Firs - average 1 ft., can be 0.5-1.5 ft./yr.
* Douglas-Fir - average 1 ft., can be 1-3 ft./yr.

* Ponderosa Pine - 1 to 3 ft./yr.
* Canadian Hemlock - 1 to 3 ft./yr.
* Lodgepole Pine - average 1 ft., can be 0.5-2 ft./yr.
* Junipers - 1 to 2 ft./yr.
* Scotch Pine - 1 to 3 ft./yr.
* Eastern White Pine - 1 to 3 ft./yr.
* Austrian Pine - 1 to 3 ft./yr.
* Norway Spruce - 1 to 3 ft./yr.
* Mondell Pine - 2 to 6 ft./yr.
* Arbor Vitae, - average 1 ft., can be 1-3 ft/yr.;
* Conifers (General) - average 1 ft., can be 0.5-2 ft/yr.

These growth rates are averages, more so to show relative comparisons with each other, but will vary considerably depending on the growing conditions and climate. Improving the growing conditions, will certainly help increase the overall growth rates. Given fairly good growing conditions, reasonable climate, watered and fertilized, you should have a good shot at getting these growth rates.

How to grow these. Simply stated, these grow best in moist well-drained fertile soils with full sun. Most soils can be alright, but plenty of water and some added fertilizer will improve their growth and survival. If your soils are rocky, heavy clay, or very sandy, then add compost or other materials mixed into the planting spot.

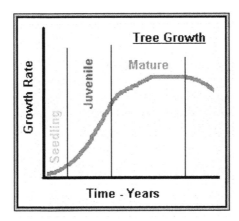

Fast growers once established, will grow very fast, then slow down after a few years. This is normally the case, and understandable from a tree competition standpoint. Pioneers especially, need plenty of light to outgrow the other trees, or they will become shaded out, reducing its survival.

TEN TREES YOU SHOULD PLANT

There are many trees to chose from, certainly each has its own merits. We came up with "our" list of ten trees, that "we" like and think will do well in most growing conditions, over the greater part of the country.

This group, the "Ten", includes:

1) Ameri-Willow Hybrid,
2) Hybrid Poplar,
3) Quaking Aspen,
4) European White Birch,
5) Red Mulberry,
6) Ohio Buckeye,
7) Red Maple,
8) Scotch Pine,
9) Douglas-Fir,
10) Norway Spruce.

To add a few alternate trees, we might add the White Willow, Horse Chestnut, Silver Maple, Northern Catalpa, Ponderosa Pine, and even the Colorado Blue Spruce. These are all unique and different, hardy, and can be planted across much of the country, under most growing conditions. More trees and notes are presented later.

1) The Ameri-Willow

One of the trees that has been planted nearly nationwide for the past twenty of so years is the Ameri-Willow. The Ameri-Willow is a hybrid, grown and produced by the Empire National Nursery, Company, and they are still found in the marketplace. It is an interesting tree, which seems to fill the need for screens and windbreaks, but also useful in the home garden as a shade tree or ornamental. Plant these in USDA Zones 4 to 10.

This tree has been popularly planted around the home for privacy screens or windbreaks. Why? Because this tree grows very fast! The average first year growth is about eight feet, and people have reported that they have had up to 15 feet of growth in the first year! If these were used for planting a live fence, would that meet the goals of speed and low cost? Growth rates will and do vary widely, and if the Ameri-Willow is half of what it may be, this tree that may well be the "fastest growing tree in America". There is no doubt that this tree grows fast!

They can grow in most types of soil and growing conditions, and as long as they get plenty of water and sun, they will grow quickly. The best conditions are a loose fertile soil, but even heavy clay or rocky soil types can be fine, but the growth rate will be slower. The keys for success are full sun, good soil, and plenty of water. These willows will drop their leaves in the fall like most broadleaf trees, but the mass of stems will add some screening during the winter months. Many people plant additional rows of the Ameri-Willow for a screen that fills in faster.

2) Hybrid Poplar

One of the most popular trees are the Hybrid Poplars. The reason is - Faster growth rates. Growth rates in good moist soil conditions can be eight feet, but its not unusual for trees to grow twelve feet or more in a single season. This means in just two or three years, the little "sticks" can become a solid wall of greenery. Only the hybrid willows are (generally) faster growing.

More insect and disease resistance. The hybrids are more resistant to many of the natural predators and pathogens, which relates to longer life and larger trees. The poplars are very interesting, and the hybrids are unique and increasingly popular and available. Another great feature is that they can be planted from Zones

2 to 9, which just about covers the whole country.

3) Quaking Aspen

For the color of its trunk, the beauty of the fall golden color, and the versatility in the landscape design, quaking aspens have become very popular. The birches are widely planted for their white trunks, but aspens are "the other white tree". They are fascinating trees, planted from USDA Zones 1 to 8.

Quaking Aspen (Populus tremuloides) is in the Poplar Family, and they are the most widely distributed tree in North America. They range from the northeastern states, all across Canada, in through Alaska, and found throughout the mountains of the western states, and into northern Mexico. They are found in a wide climatic range, with temperatures varying from -78 degrees in winter to over 100 degrees in summer. Aspens are found up to 10,000 foot elevation, where precipitation is as low as 7 inches, and a growing season barely 80 days long.

The soil conditions also vary from shallow rocky outcrops, to sandy types, to heavy clay. At high elevations, they grow in glacial outwash, shallow rock outcrops, even volcanic cinder cone soils. Much of their range is typically moist peat moss bogs. They are quick to reforest open areas caused from fires, avalanches, or heavy wind blow-downs.

Given favorable growing conditions, full sun, plenty of moisture, a little fertilizer, and a reasonable growing season, the quaking aspen will grow straight and tall very quickly. They do like water, being a poplar, and the shallow roots will spread and send up new sprouts. In the landscape design, use the tree like you would a birch - anywhere you want lines of white-trunked trees, or in clumps, or anywhere that gets a lot of visual attention. They're called quaking aspen because of the two-toned green leaves that shimmer in the breeze.

White trunks, magnificent fall gold color, an attractive tree throughout the year, makes the quaking aspen a worthwhile tree. Quaking Aspen - "the other white tree".

4) European White Birch

Very similar to the Aspen, the birch has white trunks, magnificent Fall gold coloration, and makes an attractive tree in the green screen or fence line, as well as the general landscape. Fast growth, with rates of three to four feet a year are common, and hardy, makes this a nice candidate to add to any project. The birch is planted from USDA Zones 2 to 9. More about birches is mentioned below.

5) Red Mulberry

Often not the first choice for a landscape tree, or along a driveway, in the green barrier, the mulberry is a nice addition. Fast growth and tolerance of a wide range of soils and growing conditions, the mulberry also adds sweet tasting fruit along with its fast growth rate. Good from USDA Zones 5 to 10, it is plantable over a vast part of the country. Not just a hardy fast grower, with growth rates of 3 to 4 feet year, but the roots add nitrogen to the soil. In almost every planting situation, having extra nitrogen available for the roots is desired. Either plant these in a row in between two others, and you will add fertilizer to all three rows.

6) Ohio Buckeye

Popularly planted from USDA Zones 4 to 9, the Ohio is hardy with stronger wood fibers. Perhaps slower growing than most others, rates of 2 to 3 feet a year is still a solid performance. As an inner row amongst several, the Ohio adds that solidness to a windbreak or screen. An added feature are the stalks of white flowers that produces golf ball sized nuts. This is also a nice looking shade tree that has nice autumn coloration.

7) Red Maple

Maples are often used in the windbreak or shelterbelt planting, but also good to include in other screens and barriers. Like the Ohio Buckeye, the Red makes a nice shade tree, also a hardy and solid component to any barrier. Brilliant red coloration in the Fall, with growth rates also in the 2 to 3 foot range, this tree is a also a tree with dense strong wood fibers. Plantable from USDA Zones 3 to 10, the Red is hardy of most soils and conditions.

8) Scotch Pine

Having at least one conifer in the green barrier, the Scots is one to consider. Plant these in USDA Zones 2 to 9, they also tolerate a wide range of soil and growing conditions. Growth rates once established can be in the two foot a year range, but having a year-round evergreen component in a screen adds that solid wall effect. Let it grow to a certain size, and use it for a Christmas tree should thinning out a barrier become necessary.

9) Douglas-Fir

One of the world's most important and valuable timber trees, Douglas-Fir grows extensively throughout the western US. This is the number one lumber producing tree in the US, growing in forests typified by moist fertile soils, ideal for tree growth. The tree has grown in popularity as a Christmas tree, a shelterbelt or wind-screen tree, and can also be a welcomed addition to a land-scape design. The wood is dense and heavy, making it a great for the fireplace. Plant them in USDA Zones 3 to 9.

The growth rate can vary considerably, from less than a foot to almost four feet a year. More commonly, one to two feet a year should be expected. Although native across the twelve western states, Douglas-Fir has been planted throughout the plain states in shelterbelts, and in scattered locations across the northeast as Christmas trees. Douglas-Fir, a truly beautiful tree used for many purposes.

10) Norway Spruce

Similar to the Douglas-Fir and Scotch Pine, the Norway adds a solid evergreen presence to the screen or barrier. A good Christmas tree as well, the growth rates are pretty fast for a spruce and most conifers. Growth rates of 1 to 3 feet are common, and the dense cone shape really adds that mass to a fence line or screen. Plant the Norway from USDA Zones 1 to 8, also in most soils and growing conditions.

PERFECT TREES?

Are these ten perfect trees? No. Although great trees, and good for many uses, there are some drawbacks worth mentioning. All trees and plants have some issues that arise from time to time, and these trees have them also.

Fast growing trees tend to have soft or weaker wood than slower growing types. Although the willows can break in strong gusty winds, they tend to bend. Willow wood is very elastic, used by the native peoples for bows, and you have probably heard the cliche` "bends like a willow". Still, the wood is weak and can break in severe gusty weather.

The Ameri-Willow and Poplar are not known to be root-sprouters, but the Aspen, and potentially the Mulberry, are. Like all trees, they should be planted away from water lines, sewer and septic systems, walkways, close to buildings, or any other sensitive area. All trees will send their root to seek water, and any leak in a water line would quickly en masse roots. The feeder roots are more surface oriented, and as the tree and roots grow, that can damage walkways. Always best to plan where to plant, and plan for the long-term.

Aphids and other insects may become a problem, but every tree has something that can effect it at some time. Different times of the year, different cycles of insects or leaf-eating bugs can be found. Spraying them with the appropriate pesticides is the best defense, and certainly one wants to be cautious in using such chemicals.

Deer, cows, horses, and other animals may browse the leaves. Many rural plantings are subject to deer browse, and these can get nibbled on like many plants. Deer in particular are apt to browse on varying plants particularly when the season gets dry and food becomes scarce. Also in the early spring, before other sources for nutrition is available, deer will browse on many types of trees.

The advantage with these pioneer species of trees, is the rapid growth. These are not the catch-all perfect trees, but are among the best for fast-growth and long-term stability. Consider other uses like: for wildlife habitat plantings, erosion control, noise barriers, firewood production, hedges, in landscaping plans, and even for shade.

OTHER FAST-GROWING HARDWOODS - NOTES AND INFORMATION

Aside from the Ten, there are many other trees that can be planted and used as privacy screens or for windbreaks. More willows, Poplars, Horse Chestnut, other birches, maples, spruces, cypress, even fruit trees, are just a few to ponder. What to plant, in what combination, how fast will they grow, and how each can fit in a particular set of growing conditions, makes for some challenging questions. Growth rates is a complex factor of climate and growing conditions, and they interact with each tree species. Every tree or shrub will respond differently in different parts of the country. That is pretty clear to understand that, as most gardeners and farmers well know.

Among the best and fastest growing trees are a class called "Pioneers". A pioneer tree, whether an individual species, or an entire genus, has a very common characteristic, they grow fast. Pioneers in forest succession are those trees that are first to colonize new ground. New ground, meaning that which is created either by flood, fire, or other catastrophic event, that clears the ground for the seeds to sprout and become established. The trees grow fast, fighting for sunlight, water, and nutrients, before another tree crowds them out. In this long-term process, the pioneers "work the ground", so to speak, preparing it for other trees and plants to seed in and eventually replace them. In the natural world, this series of successional growth and replacement can take decades or longer. The obvious analogy is how this country developed where pioneers would go into the wilderness, scratch out farms and homes, which later became settlements, towns, then cities.

The plant Family, Salicaceae, includes a large number of popularly planted fast-growers, including the Willows, Poplars, and Aspens. The Willows are in the Salix genus, and the Poplars are in the Populus genus, which includes the Aspens. The willows and poplars are very fast growing, with a lot of variation among the species, but growth rates can reach five to ten feet a year initially, then slows down. Lifespans are relatively short for trees, anywhere from a few decades, up to 80 years (in general). Many individual trees in the various species can live to be over a hundred years, but overall, consider them as short-lived.

OTHER HYBRID WILLOWS

The planting of hybrid trees has become the way of the plant industry, and the desire for faster and better growing trees has prompted the breeding of the hybrid willows.

The hybrid tree-forms also are very rapid growers, with growth rates varying from four to reportedly fifteen a year! This can vary dramatically based on planting conditions, climate, and timing. Water, full sun, and rich well-drained soils are the keys to the fastest growth. Because the willows are hardy, they can tolerate very poor heavy soils to very sterile sandy soils. Supplementing water and fertilizer is therefore desirable for the best performance. Because they are hybrids, they are sterile, and therefore don't produce the cottony seeds like the true natives. Tree shapes can vary also, from broad shade-tree like, to box-like hedge types, to cascading pendant branching trees.

Of the over 200 species of Willows native to the northern hemisphere, about 30 are native to the United States. The willows are found from the Arctic Circle as low-growing shrub types, all the way south to the warmest sub-tropical areas. The willow genus Salix is divided into two broad groups - the Trees, and the Shrubs. And the Family Salixaceae also includes the Poplars, Cottonwoods, and Aspens.

There are some big advantages in planting the hybrids ornamentally. The key factor is the rapid growth, and the planting of them for privacy screens seems to be the most popular usage. They are easily trimmed and maintained, and can be grown as a hedge or single shade trees, which makes them versatile. Since they are sterile, they are relatively clean, and their shallow root systems tend to be free of sprouting or spreading. As a windbreak, the hybrids can be used, having a wood fiber that is very shock resistant, even though the wood is light weight and breakable. The cliché "bends like a willow" is appropriate here. The long narrow leaves and dark green color make for an attractive plant as well.

MORE ABOUT WILLOWS

The genus is Salix, and has over 200 species, most of which are native to the northern hemisphere. There are about 30 species that are "trees" in the United States, and there are a many varieties among these.

The whole genus and family is characteristically found around streams and low-lying areas where the supply of water is abundant. The willows are pioneers, being the first to colonize bare ground, which often is along the stream banks after the winter storms have cleared new ground. The seeds, like the tiny tufts of cotton that the Cottonwoods produce, carries the seeds by air and water to fresh ground where they quickly establish. Whether tree-form or shrub-form, the initial
growth is fast, about the fastest of any genus of tree. It is typical for first year seedlings to grow four to six feet or more when planted naturally like this.

Some of the more popularly planted willows -
* Ameri-Willow
* Green Weeping Willow
* Niobe Weeping Willow
* Black Willow
* White Willow
* Coastal Willow
* Flame Willow
* Purple Osier Willow

* Laurel Willow
* Coyote Willow
* French Pussy Willow
* Corkscrew Willow
* Sandbar Willow
* Bankers Willow

Black Willow

Black Willow (Salix nigra), is a native tree, almost what you would call a generic willow. It is the average of what willows look like, if that makes any sense. The Black is naturally found from southern Maine to northern Mexico, along creeks and low areas where water collects. It can vary from 10 to 40 feet tall, USDA Zones 2 to 10. So if you get a chance, go visit a creekside and you may find them.

Weeping Willow

The Weeping Willow is a fast growing and majestic tree. Growth can be 6 to 8 feet or more a year. As the tree gets large, the long thin pendant branches hang down, creating a flowing umbrella of best use for these are in wet areas, or where they can be the yard centerpiece or specimen. It is important to keep weeping willows away from sewer lines, or other underground pipes.

The Coastal Willow

The Coastal Willow, also called the Florida or Swamp Willow, is found from North Carolina to the tip of the Everglades swamp. The climate is mild to warm in the winters, and abundant water is where they are found. these can be trained into a small tree, but they are more of a tall shrub.

White Willow

Although not greatly known in this country, the White Willow is widely planted throughout Europe, and can be planted from USDA Zones 2 to 10. The fast growth makes it a nice choice for the landscape design, especially for screens and windbreaks, and for wetter soils as well. Tall and hardy, with yellow stems and trunks when younger, these are an attractive choice for a variety of uses.

Pussy Willows

The favorite of many craft people are the French Pussy Willow and the Corkscrew Willow. These small trees will get 15-25 feet tall, and tolerates Zone 4 to 10. The key feature with the Pussy Willow is the large fuzzy buds as the tree begins to leaf out, and the curly twisty stems on the Corkscrew. Other than for dry arrangements, they do well in wet areas as a specimen tree. They can be a border, especially for low-lying wet areas. There are other species of Pussy Willow, like the Pink and the Japanese.

Black Willow

The Black Willow, is native to the eastern half of the country. It is a fast growing hardy tree up to 70 feet tall. A good choice for privacy screens and as a shade tree in Zones 4 to 10, these can get 12-20 feet wide.

Corkscrew Willow

Lesser know in the landscape design The Corkscrew Willow stems are popular among craft and hobby folks as an interesting twisty floral item. It is a decorative tall shrub to medium sized tree, good for Zones 5 to 10, as an ornamental specimen, hedges and privacy screens, or as shade tree. Fast growth with the young stems in a spiral or "corkscrew" shape.

THE HYBRID POPLARS

Over the past several years, we had some of the other Hybrid Poplars. As production and supplies of sellable plants increases, we will again offer other hybrids. For a number of years, our primary "Hybrid Poplar" was the Eastern Cottonwood, also called the Siouxland Poplar (Populus deltoides v. deltoides). This is plantable almost nationwide, and performs well in growth rate, survival, form, and durability.

The Newer Hybrids

* Imperial Carolina Poplar (Populus canadensis v. Imperial)
* Prairie Sky Poplar (Populus canadensis v. Prairie Sky)
* Norway Poplar (Populus v. Norway)
* Cottonless Cottonwood (Populus canadensis v. Robusta)
* Androscoggin Poplar (Populus spp.)

Eastern Cottonwood (Siouxland Poplar) - Very fast growth, gets up to 80 feet tall in Zone 3 to 10. They need full sun, are non-suckering (supposedly), but are versatile as screens, fence lines, or as shade trees.

The differences between these new poplars and our standard Siouxland is basically that they are more narrow in shape, resembling the Lombardy in many cases. Need a narrower fast-growing poplar, then any of these might work also.

Lombardy Poplar (Theves Poplar) - Very fast growth, gets up to 80 feet tall. these are hardy from Zones 2 to 10, also need full sun, very tight column shape, making them great for fence lines and narrow spaces. Some of the Lombardy Poplars are also hybrids, being the Theves Poplar (Populus nigra v. thevestina), or the Afghan Poplar (Populus nigra v. afghanica).

The Horse Chestnut

Actually a native to the Balkans of southern Europe, the Horse Chestnut is widely planted throughout the United States. A member of the Horse Chestnut Family (Hippocastanaceae), the Horse (Aesculus hippocastanum) is just one of some 25 or so species in the buckeye genus. These are an attractive showy shade tree.

Similar to the other Buckeyes, the Horse has an opposite palmately compound deciduous leaf composed of five to seven elliptical leaflets, varying from 4 to 10 inches long and 2 to 3.5 inches wide, yet distinctly widest near the abruptly pointed apex. The showy flowers are creamy-white tubular or bell-shaped, with marks of red or yellow, borne in erect panicles eight to twelve inches long in early spring. By the fall, the tree is covered with round spiny 3-parted capsules almost three inches in size. Usually one and sometimes two, the seed is a huge shiny chocolate brown with a light-colored hilum resembling an "eye", hence the name buckeye. The seeds are not edible, which is too bad, they are meaty. Mowing the lawn in the fall is sometimes difficult and painful since the "eyes" are pitched by mowers blade.

Horse Chestnuts are medium sized trees varying from 25 to 60 feet tall, with a medium to wide- spreading crown. These have been very popularly grown since as early as 1576 throughout the southern European region. Here, they are often planted in parks or along streets for shade and their showy flowers. Being relatively free from pests, and growing from half shade to full sun, down to Zone 4, the Horse Chestnut is a nice choice for shade. With plenty of moisture, two to three feet of growth can occur on most soil types, although they prefer the deeper better soils. These make a worthwhile tree to have in the landscape design.

OTHER BIRCH TREES

Without question, one of the most popular trees for the home and landscape design is the white-trunked birch. There are only a few trees that have such an elegant and clean-looking white appearance, which is a welcomed contrast to the greens and browns of summer foliage. For the same reason Quaking Aspen is popular, along with Sweetgum and Alder to a lesser extent. But the birch is the most popular because of the wide range of plant zones and planting conditions, and the many hybrid varieties that are available.

The genus is "Betula", and are part of the Birch Family (Betulaceae), which has over 100 members (the birches having about 40 species), and includes Alders (Alnus), Hornbeams (Carpinus), Hophornbeams (Ostrya), and Hazelnuts (Corylus). Most noted other characteristics are the small round leaves with jagged or serrated edges, and the birch seed-cones, called strobili. Those little brown hanging seed holders that fall apart when the seeds get ripe.

The birches are planted nationwide, in almost all plant zones, and naturally found throughout USDA Zones 2 to 8. They are typically in areas that are cool and moist, needing that extra water when the weather gets warm and dry.

They are popular because of their versatility in the landscape plan. The size is small to medium, with 50 to 60 feet being common. They have shallow root systems that are generally not intrusive or destructive, but large trees can have large surface roots. Birches can be planted close to the house or buildings, a stand alone accent in the yard, and used to contrast other plants or building characteristics. Birch are not a good shade tree, they tend to have a medium-tight shape and small leaves. The most popular use is to plant birch in lines such as along a fence line or driveway. They are planted an average of six feet apart, but that can vary according to preference.

The birch clump is a very popular way to fill an area or create visual interest. Their is a debate whether to plant three trees (average number) close together to make a clump, or one multi-stem tree. It is a personal preference and the result is about the same. The growth rate of planting three trees is more even and they get bigger faster, but the multiple stem tree adds a very natural look.

There are about 40 natural species of birch, but many hybrids. The most popularly grown birches are:

(White-trunked Birches)
* European White Birch, grows up to 80 feet
* Paper Birch, 60 to 90 feet
* Jacmonti Birch, 50 to 80 feet
* Whitespire Birch, 50 to 80 feet
* Japanese White Birch, 50 to 60 feet
* Monarch Birch, 50 to 80 feet
* River Birch, 40 to 50 feet
* Gray Birch, 25 to 30 feet

(Other Non-White Birches)
* Yellow Birch, grows 60 to 80 feet
* Gold Birch, 50 to 60 feet
* Water Birch, 20 to 25 feet
* Sweet Birch, 50 to 60 feet
* Bog Birch, 10 to 20 feet

They grow fairly fast once they get established, up to several feet a year. They add beauty and value like no other tree, and birch firewood is the best! There is a minor problem that devastates birches - the Bronze Birch Borer (Agrilis anxius). There are more trees that killed and deformed from this beetle than any other pest for birches in the landscape design. What the borer does is tunnel into stems and girdles the living tissue. Soon, your tree has a dead branch, then another, and eventually the tree is gone.

There are a couple things to do. First, cut off the dead or dying branches and "burn" them. The tunneled stems are full of eggs and beetles, and burning them is the only effective treatment to get rid of them. Trees should next be sprayed with Lindane, which is now not found in your local garden center. If you can find Lindane, wear long sleeves, gloves, eye protection, and wash up diligently afterwards. Safety first with Lindane, you won't get a second chance, because it is a very toxic and deadly chemical. By the way, Lindane is about the only available chemical to kill borers, bark beetles, and weevils. The key therefore is to maintain healthy trees.

If you had a birch die from borers, does it mean you can't have birch trees? No. The borers are attracted to "weak" trees. Simply natures design - healthy trees resist insects and disease. Weak trees are attacked, and its a matter of "survival of the fittest". This is basically what happens with the birch borer.

The cause is usually the roots. The roots are the key to trees. Birch have a natural occurrence of "die-back" in the winter. Sometimes, the branches or twigs naturally die back, due in part to the harshness of the winter weather. This condition can weaken the trees, and attract borers. In the home landscape design, tree roots are weakened by lack of watering, and soil temperatures getting too hot. The natural environment is down to Zone 2, and planted in warm climates, the summer heat causes too much warmth of the soil surface, and weakens the tree roots. The beetles sense that, and attack the trees.

Because the birch have shallow roots, keep them watered during the summer months, do add fertilizer once in a while, and where practical, have a mulch layer. A several inch layer of mulch will protect the soil surface from getting hot, and hence keeps the roots moist and healthy. Mulch can be a layer of bark or leaves. Plant a groundcover around the trees which will become a "live mulch", and add beauty to the landscape design. Either way, mulching is important for birches.

The medium narrow shape, the clean look, the elegance, and beautiful yellow leaves in the fall, Birch trees adds more value to the property than any other plant.

NOTES ON MORE FAST GROWERS

With reasonably good growing conditions, other broadleafs can grow fast as well. Paulownia is also a pioneer genus, with very fast growth, rivaling the willows and poplars. There are several species in the genus, with the Empress Tree (Paulownia tomentosa) being widely planted. Interesting how this oriental tree originated in this country, from the seed pods used as packing materials. Fine china and other goods, notably from Japan, would be packed using the woody seed pods, then the pods would be discarded outside once unpacked. Now the Paulownia is more often planted for the stalks of fragrant showy purple flowers, not so much planted for screens.

Sycamores, Sweetgum, Honey and Black Locusts, Tulip Tree, Birch, and Silver Maple, are fast growers that are used more so in windbreak plantings than green fences. The difference between these more common broadleaf trees, and the Salix pioneers is the width of the trees as they grow. In general, the broadleafs tend to be grow wider, shade-tree like, whereas the willows and poplars tend to be more narrow and columnar in growth habit. If space is available for the broadleafs, they can be used for screens or fences, but they have a more practical use for windbreaks. Other broadleaf tree species can be used for screens and fences as well, all of which have varying rates of growth.

The Paulownia, has fast growth when they are young, and except for the clusters of purple flowers on the Paulownia, their best use is for borders and fence lines, or areas where they can freely fill in the bare ground.

These include, but not limited to these trees -
* Cherry Laurel
* Black Locust
* Thornless Honey Locust
* Northern Catalpa
* Russian Olive
* American Sycamore
* Sweetgum
* Paulownia - Empress
* European White Birch
* Black Cherry
* Black Walnut
* Kentucky Coffeetree
* Tulip Tree
* Ailanthus (Tree of Heaven)
* Siberian Elm
* Pin Oak
* Red Mulberry
* Silver Maple

There are many others as well.

The Sweetgum (Liquidamber)

Few trees are more spectacular than the Sweetgum. The American Sweetgum or Red Gum is found from the southern tip of New York, across the Ohio and Mississippi valleys, and across the southern states from eastern Texas to northern Florida. The Gum, Sycamore Gum, Alligator Tree, Gumwood, Starleaf Gum, or Sapgum are all referring to the lone Sweetgum, the sole member of the Genus Liquidamber (species is styraciflua). At least it is in North America, with 3 or 4 cousins in Asia. The Gum is a member of the slightly larger Witch-Hazel Family, Hamamelidaceae.

The Sycamore Gum has sycamore-like star-shaped leaves that have a sweet pungent order when crushed. The tell-tail characteristic of the Alligator Tree is the spiny ball seed capsule it forms.

The most popular trait of the Sweetgum is the rainbow colors it makes in the fall. They change from medium green to yellow and gold, then to orange and red, then scarlet and maroon, and finally to the purple shades. How many trees have so many colors? Ok, we added a few, but they make the wide band, and a single tree often has a mix of all of the colors at the same time. They are really a sight!

One of the nice features of the Gum is they grow better on heavy poorly drained soils, and they can grow fairly fast, up to three or four feet a year after they get established. Not bad for a tree that likes heavy soils.

They like full sun and a fair amount of water, so using them in the landscape, they are good for lines, and areas where space is limited and the fall colors will get a lot of attention. The branches are not wide spreading, but the roots are. They will sprout, and gum up the pipes if given the chance. Other than that, the Gum is a hardy tree, has few pests and sturdy wood.

The trees live long, and can reach over 100 feet tall, but not any time soon, so plant them for fall color, it is a rainbow of a pretty tree.

Paulownia (Princess or Empress Tree)

Many trees come and go as fads, and the Paulownia is one those. There are several species of Paulownia (P. elongata, P. fortunei, P. kawakamii, P. tomentosa), all native to China, and have been planted in the US for many years. There are several other names for this tree, Royal Paulownia, Empress Tree, and Princess Tree are among them. They are rated as Zone 6, found from New York to western Texas, and along the Pacific coast states. The south-eastern states seem to have quite a lot planted also.

What's popular about the Paulownia is that they grow very fast, and have large ten inch long masses of fragrant violet to dark blue flowers that come out between April and May. They tend to be medium sized trees, where the P. kawakamii gets up to 30 to 40 feet, and the P. tomentosa gets 40 to 60 feet tall. The P. elongata is used as a timber tree in China, and gets upwards of 100 feet tall.

In the landscape design, these are planted as shade trees, in places where they can spread out. As members of the Trumpet Creeper Family (Bignoniaceae), the leaves are large and almost heart-shaped. The Catalpa's are close relatives. The growth rate is very fast, and the shade they produce is very dense, perfect for those hot summer days.

These are great shade trees, fast growing, and produces fragrant flowers. They are the perfect tree? Well, maybe not. After the flowers fade, the seed capsules are formed. With almost 3 million seeds per pound, they tend to spread - everywhere. If the temperature is warm, then they can germinate in about ten days. Potentially a gardening nightmare.

Something that seems to be really odd with this tree is that it takes a few years for it to become a tree. It grows really fast, but at the end of the season, it dies. It acts like a large sunflower, rapid growth, great flower, but when its done, its a weed. It seems to take several years to get out of this stage and finally become tree-like. Still, that they are a Princess of a tree. What do you think?

FAST GROWING SHRUBS

For many fence projects, trees are just too tall. One of the goals of a green fence is to delineate a property boundary, and forty or fifty foot trees just may not be practical at all. Shorter trees can be used, but slower growth rates and growth habit might not be the best fit. There are some shrubs that can offer fairly rapid growth, and if there are height restrictions, these might work nicely, especially if local ordinances or rules are in place.

Privets are popularly used for screens and windbreaks, so are the Red-Tip Photinia, lilacs, dogwoods, and other types. Lines planted with roses and many other shrubs are used, again depending on the goal or purpose of the fence. Like using trees, there are a number of factors in selecting what to plant. The shrubs overall can offer moderate to fairly quick growth, which may work for some fencing or screening projects. But shrubs offer the shorter heights that can fit better for many projects.

FAST-GROWING CONIFERS (EVERGREENS)

Which Conifers are Fast-Growing? Usually not as dramatic in growth rates as the hardwoods, some conifers or evergreens can quickly gain some size. Here again, understanding the basic environmental factors, the growth can be increased.

If the plan is to plant a fast growing tree for screens, then why not just plant evergreens? Sure, evergreens can be planted instead of going with the broadleafs, especially as a screens effectiveness is lessened during the winter months. The answer is time. The pioneers grow faster, establish a live barrier quicker, quicker than any of the evergreens. Still, planted in combination with the pioneers, a privacy screen or barrier can become highly effective year round.

If there are faster growing evergreens, then the Pine Family (Pinaceae) has the bulk of them. Most of the faster growers are the Pines, in the Pinus genus. Some pines grow very slowly, others, pretty quickly, with a lot of variation in between. Overall, the Scotch Pine, Ponderosa, Mondell, and White Pine (to a lesser extent) can grow one to three feet a year, maybe more once established. The Norway Spruce is the fastest growing of the spruces, with similar growth rates on average.

Some of these conifers that can grow faster includes: Leyland Cypress, Coast Redwood, Canadian Hemlock, Mondell Pine, Scotch Pine, and Ponderosa Pine. Although not really very fast, the Arbor Vitae can grow pretty quickly. They vary in growth rates, but 2 to 4 feet or more can be achieved, and even faster on some species. Some of the Cypress species, like the Leyland Cypress, can grow three or more feet a year. Cryptomeria is a little known fast growing evergreen, again like the pines in growth rates. Coast Redwood can be a very fast grower in good moist conditions, highly variable depending on conditions. Hemlock can also grow fast, another good choice for an evergreen.

A couple other conifers that grow fast are the Dawn Redwood and the Larches. Growth rates are like the pines. Because they make cones, they are conifers, but unlike the other conifers, these are not evergreen, but deciduous like the broadleaf trees.

Overall, the evergreens have a number of good plantable trees that can be used for screens and fences, but the growth rates are much slower, and that is after they become somewhat established.

Take for instance the Coast Redwood. In its natural surroundings, the foggy cool climate of the California north coast, these trees growth rather slowly. Young trees in full shade may grow a few inches a year. In full sun, with good soils, with a bit more moisture, growth rates of 4 to 6 feet a year are more common. The differences have a lot to do with more moisture, more sunlight, and higher nutrient levels in the soil. The climate where they are planted is a key consideration as the Redwoods don't tolerate cold or dry too well.

Now contrast the cool moist requirements of the redwood, with the fast growth of the Leyland Cypress or Mondell Pine. Both of these trees are also not very tolerant of the cold climates, but they don't like the cool wetness either. These two conifers grow best under warm dry conditions, and growth rates can be as high as 4 to 6 feet a year! Given sufficient water, they will grow very well in the dry regions, whereas most other trees won't!

Are there fast growing conifers that grow in the colder zones? Yes. Understand, there is a relationship between the Plant Zone and the length of the growing season. Also, the colder the zone, the less time a tree has to grow, and the conifers seem to grow even slower. The broadleaf trees like the willows and poplars seem to grow fast even in the colder zones, but the conifers are just slower than usual! There are four trees to consider - the Canadian Hemlock, the Scotch Pine, the Ponderosa Pine, and even the Arbor Vitae.

The Canadian Hemlock grows well in the colder zones, under shade or full sun conditions, but they do need a fair amount of water. The Scotch Pine, although not a very fast grower, also grows well in the colder, wet climates, like the hemlock. The Ponderosa also not a greatly fast grower, does grow fairly quick in the colder drier zones than the warm-zone conifers. The Arbor Vitae would not be considered a fast grower by our standards, but they are widely planted from the colder wet and dry zones, to the hot reaches of Zone 10!

Many people plant a row of faster growing hardwood trees to provide a quicker screen, along with a row of slower growing conifers. There are so many different situations across the country, but there are fast growing conifers that can be planted.

Throughout the south and western states where the climate is hot and dry, or in many of the northern plains where it is cold and dry, year-round screening is highly desirable, but the fast-growing tree options are few. Plant the Junipers! Can't plant anything else, the Junipers are typically hardy of the worst growing conditions, especially the heat and very limited moisture. Granted the growth rates of one to two feet a year is not fast-growing per se, but if its very difficult to get anything else established, the Junipers are the tree to plant.

And not all Evergreens are Conifers. There are not many broadleaf hardwoods that retain their leaves, but those few are evergreens. Trees like the Southern Magnolia, Waxleaf Privet (growing up to 20 feet tall), English Laurel, Red-Tip Photinia, are a few that also make great candidates for screens and barriers.

Colorado Blue Spruce

One of the most popular conifer trees to plant as a specimen or in a fence line is the blue spruce. For obvious reasons, it is rare to have a bluish colored tree.

The Colorado Blue Spruce (Picea pungens) is a member of the Pine Family (Pinaceae), and the natural range is in the Colorado Rocky Mountains. They are found at the higher elevations from 6,000 to over 10,000 feet, either in dense stands or as scattered individuals. In the past, it was used as a timber tree, especially as the mountain area was being developed, but since then, it is a minor timber species. The tree is slow growing, from a few inches a year, to maybe a foot or more if the conditions are good.

Since the introduction into the ornamental landscaping market, the blue spruce has become very popular. They are expensive trees to buy, related to the slow growth, but also to the uniqueness of the tree. There are now about twenty varieties of this tree, but basically its still a blue spruce.

Use this tree to highlight a key area in the yard, where the tree is the focal point of that area. You can also plant a line of spruces, along a fence, driveway, as a screen or other border. As they get bigger, the visual impact is stunning, and the value of the property is greatly enhanced.

They grow tall, but slowly, and not wide spreading like a hardwood, so for general planning, use one foot of growth per year. If you start with a one foot tall seedlings, then generally, in ten years, that tree will be about ten feet tall. A five foot tall tree, in another five years, would be about ten feet tall. This is just a general rule, varies of course, but in making landscaping decisions, this is worthwhile.

WHAT WILL THESE TREES DO?

As a planting project comes together and plans are being formulated, the designs and tree selections are being made. But what are some of the goals or desires of selecting various trees? The need is to plant trees that will screen or become a windbreak, and fast growth is among the primary goals. Whether a project is planted using the ten trees we suggest, or others among the trees noted, there are other benefits that will happen.

1) Fast growth - 3' to 8' in the first year. Growth rates will vary due to site conditions, climate, planting time, and other factors. Nationwide first-year average seems to be about eight feet, but past customers have reported first-year growth from three to six feet, and others have stated over ten feet. The first five years are the fastest growing years, then the trees tend to slow down and branch out until mature. You can expect your trees to slow down in growth after the first five years, but they should be anywhere from 30 to 50 feet tall. They will live up to 70 years or more, and grow from 50 up to 90 feet tall. They generally grow about 10-15 feet wide. Height, width, and growth rates are highly variable, so this is general information.

2) Fast Privacy - As a privacy screen, the fast growth will be tall and dense, making a solid wall of greenery within a few years. They will naturally branch out and fill in, so you don't need to trim. Planted in a line about six feet apart, the growing limbs will intermingle. The total width of the tree will be about ten to

twelve feet wide, but allowed to grow in the open by itself, it may become wider. The Ameri-Willow will drop its leaves in the fall like most other broadleaf trees, so year-round screening, consider planting a row of evergreens close by. The two rows will eventually become a year-year solid wall.

3) The Ten are pretty hardy and fairly disease resistant, and tolerant to most climates, and most soils. They will take the high humidity and heat of the south, and survive the winters of Zone 4. They grow best from Zones 5 to 9, and can do well.

4) Long Life - These trees will live up to 70 years or more.

5) Excellent for windbreaks and shelter belts - Effective wind and dust barriers in the first year. The thicker the wind barrier, the more effective it will become against the wind. Plant several rows, including a row of evergreens, and tall shrubs or other broadleafs.

6) Great for erosion protection - As they grow very fast, they stabilize the soil against wind and water erosion. The root system will spread out which holds the soil in place. Do add a surface mulch like straw or other materials to reduce rain and moving-water effects.

7) Living snow fence - planted as a fence in areas of blowing snow, they will trap and hold the snow. Although the stems will be barren during the winter months, they will act as a snow fence helping to trap drifting snow.

8) Easy and hardy to grow - Once they are planted, they require very little care. Just keep them watered during the dry periods, and add fertilizer a couple times during the season.

How many other uses can you find for these amazing trees? They can work great for wildlife habitat, noise barriers, firewood production, hedges, in landscaping plans, and even for shade.

MAKE IT GROW FASTER: IMPROVE THE GROWTH

You Can Increase the Growth Rate of Your Trees! Not that this is a thorough and absolute list, but these ideas are practical and easy to undertake. The results will vary of course, but you will at least increase your knowledge, and enhance the health of your plants.

Plants react to the environmental surroundings, and either they will do well, grow fairly well, or will be under a stressed condition. Briefly stated are these points to consider:

1) Know Your Plant Zone;
2) Know Your Soil;
3) Water is Life;
4) Fertilizer;
5) Sunlight and Planting Location;
6) Mulch and Weed Control;
7) Pests, Pathogens, and Animals;
8) Selecting Quality Trees and Plants.

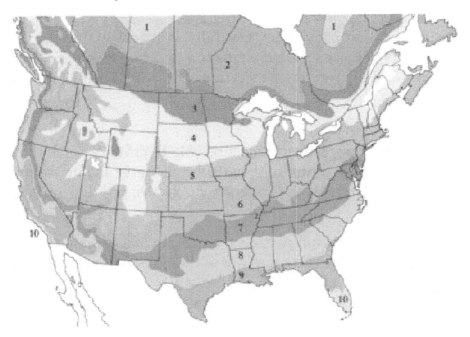

Do You Know Your Plant Zone?

Different plants grow in different areas of the world, and many plants will grow do fine almost anywhere, but others can only be planted in selected areas. How do you make sense of it all?

The United States Department of Agriculture (USDA), and others, have developed a basic map to show "zones", of similar climates in the United States. Many books, such as the Sunset Garden Book, have categorized most plants into a "zone classification".

Thereby, if you simply look on the map, you will learn what climate zone you're in. Then when shopping for trees and plants, usually through books such as Sunset, then you can find out its zone classification.

The whole point of this is to match plants that suitable to your area. If you plant a tropical plant in the north east, you will find that the first cold spell will kill the plant. Knowing the zone, you can avoid most of these setbacks.

The trees our company offers, "generally" will do well throughout the country. If you ever have a question about a particular plant, and can't find any answers, do feel free to drop us a note.

Know Your Soil

In order for a tree to live, it must be able to grow its roots into the soil, where the feeder roots will absorb water and nutrients. That's pretty obvious, but understanding basic soil dynamics is critical.

Soil is composed of soil particles, water, air, and organic materials. There are many combinations of these ingredients that will make your soil "like a brick", easy to work, or be very loose. It is this soil composition that allows water to easily soak into the ground, hold water, or maybe not allow water in at all.

This is exactly why people add soil mixes or manure, or grass clippings, or other organic materials to their soil. A "good" soil is a balance of the ingredients, whereby the plant grows well, looks healthy, and flourishes.

Always keep in mind "the balance". Too much heavy soil, means there is not enough organic materials to break up the clods. The result is not enough air and water is getting inside. Too muck rock or sand, a very loose soil, suggests not enough soil particles and/or organic materials to hold enough water and nutrients. A workable soil may allow enough water and air to move through, but if it lacks organic materials, then there could be a lack of fertilizer or nutrient cycling.

The whole concept is like a wheel, well balanced and linked to the other ingredients. Tree growth will improve with a well-balanced soil. If fact, most plants prefer a "good" soil.

Water is Life

Without water, nothing lives. The extremes are very simple to understand, the desert versus the swamp. Part of the soil composition is water. How much to have in the soil is almost unanswerable. It is clear when there is enough... the plant doesn't wilt. Having too much can make a plant wilt too (rot is better word to use here). Trees use more water than bedding plants, that is clear also. The bigger the plant, the larger the roots system, therefore it uses more water. Fast-growing trees tend to use a lot of water. Either they are planted in areas that are naturally wet, or extra water is needed, such as with a sprinkler system.

Some people like to use timers on a sprinkler or drip-system, others hand water, and there are many ways to keep the trees and plants moist. Your climate is a big factor as well. The drier and southern climates will require more watering, whereas the northern or rainy areas may not need very much extra watering. So how long to water and when, has to be decided by you looking at the plants and the ground.

Fertilizing

There is a lot of uncertainty about when to fertilize, but here also, fertilizing is pretty simple. Fertilizer is fertilizer, but as it comes in a number of forms, and almost an infinite variety of strengths or nutrient combinations, so the usage can be beneficial or detrimental to seedlings and newly planted trees. So the question is "what type", "how often", and "how much".

Firstly, do not fertilize at the time of planting. Let the plants get settled in for a month or so before sprinkling a light fertilizer on the soil surface. Then when fertilizer is added, do water afterwards. This helps to rinse whatever might have gotten onto the plant leaves or stems, and then keeps it from washing away (as from storms). It also waters in the nitrogen, which can partly evaporate. Make sure the plants are watered well after fertilizing, also to reduce the chance of "burning" the feeder roots.

It is worthwhile to understand basic fertilizer. Typically, and probably due to packaging legalities, fertilizer is noted as an N-P-K strength rating, expressed as a percentage. 6-10-4 is a common fertilizer, saying the Nitrogen is 6%, the Phosphorus is 10%, and the Potassium is 4% in
concentration. Many fertilizers, such as Miracle Grow or Peter's Plant Food list many of the minor nutrients and minerals in addition to the N-P-K, making these types similar to a multi-vitamin. Of all of the minerals, it is the three major nutrients that are the most important, and heavily used by the plants.

There organic fertilizers such as fish emulsion, compost, and bone meal, and then inorganic or man-made types such as the 6-10-4. Fertilizer can be a fast-release water soluble type like Miracle Grow and Peter's (two of the most popular brands), or slower-release granular forms. There are fertilizers for general use, or specific formulations to aide in blooming, types for certain plants, lawn fertilizers, and many other blends. Fertilizers can be highly concentrated, very low amounts of NPK, and every combination in between.

Nitrogen is the key and most important element, primarily coming from the atmosphere and highly soluble. Nitrogen has to do with amino acid development, chloroplast production, leaf production, and overall growth. It also helps to release or "make available" the other nutrients for the roots. In other words, nitrogen is a catalyst, so if nothing else, add nitrogen. Leaf litter and compost when used as a mulch layer is a good slow-release source of nitrogen and all of the other nutrients, which is partly why mulching is highly recommended.

Phosphorus is a low water soluble mineral, found in almost all soils in moderate amounts. Phosphorus for seedlings and small trees is the lesser of importance here, since it aides in flower production, and other processes. Choosing a fertilizer with low amounts of phosphorus is fine, but not a major concern.

Potassium is highly soluble found in most soils, and probably the second key ingredient you ideally want for the first several fertilizings. Potassium has to do with root development, and roots are the key to a trees' growth, especially after transplanting. A strong root system will result in stronger top-growth and overall health.

Within the basic ingredients of a soil mix, the organic materials and the soil particles are basically composed of nutrients that help the plant grow well. Water will hold and transport dissolved nutrients either into the soil, or out of the soil. There are also nutrients in the air, that eventually become plant materials, such as carbon (being the most important). Remember the air we breathe is composed of nitrogen, hydrogen, carbon compounds, and many other elements and particulate in addition to oxygen.

Like a good balanced soil, a "good" balance of nutrients, will result in faster growth and healthier plants. What type of fertilizer is the best? Basically, fertilizer is fertilizer. Some are granules, some powders, and some are mixed with water, some are slow release and others are fast release. Fertilizer packaging points to the amount of nitrogen-phosphorus-potassium (N-P-K,), the major nutrients. If a fertilizer is a 10-6-4, it says there is a ratio of those three nutrients, expressed as a percentage (10%-6%-4%). The higher the number, the stronger the fertilizer. The stronger the fertilizer, the greater the chance of "burning" shallow-rooted plants.

When a nutrient is lacking, then the plant reacts to it. Most commonly, as a basic principle, when nitrogen is lacking in the soil, the plant turns yellowish. Trees that grow fast will likely run out of nitrogen before the other nutrients. Therefore, having enough organic materials in the soil, and occasionally adding fertilizer, the growth will not be hindered.

When to fertilize? Fertilize all trees and shrubs at least twice, in late winter or early spring, then again in late spring or early summer. Both fertilizations should be high in nitrogen, as that is the key nutrient, and that which will have the greatest demand. During the growing season, when the tree leaves start to turn yellow, that is usually a sign of nitrogen deficiency, but use a well balanced type to assure the best results. If possible, a light or low-strength monthly fertilizing assures a steady supply of nutrients for the roots. The growth process demands a lot of nitrogen, singly the best nutrient, and any fertilizer can work fine. You might consider something like Miracle-Grow or Peter's, and even lawn fertilizer that is high in nitrogen. The added nitrogen will help the other soil nutrients become more available, and also hastens the breakdown of organic material.

What type of fertilizer to use, a commonly misunderstood part about gardening and plants. Basically, there are two types of fertilizer, 'organic", and "inorganic". Organic means not man made, and inorganic means is was created in a factory, so to speak. Although an organic type may have more of the trace minerals or micro nutrients present, understand that "fertilizer is fertilizer is fertilizer", it is all the same. That is, the main three basic components of all fertilizer (unless a specially made blend), includes Nitrogen, Phosphorus, and potassium (K, the elemental initial for potassium), in that order, N-P-K. On organic or inorganic packages, there should be a stated ratio of these three nutrients, expressed in percentages. Some packaging also shows what micro nutrients might be present.

There is water soluble and granular types. Those that can be mixed and dissolved in water are fine, as is the type you scatter by hand.

Now which to use in the garden, landscape, or a tree farm, depends on ones preference. If an organic type is readily available and meets a budget or other plan, then use organic. If there is a sale at the store on a bag of an inorganic type, perhaps select that. Once in the ground, the soil bacteria will convert it to a usable form for the roots to absorb. At that point, organic versus inorganic, and the percentages of each, all become a mute point. They are all good, and often you have to just use what you can best make use of.

For seedlings and trees that were transplanted, allow several weeks for initial establishment before adding anything. Even poor soils have some nutrients that will help feed the plant, and the important consideration during this time is keeping the roots moist (but not wet). Afterwards, you
can start with a water soluble type, such as Miracle Grow or Peter's to give the tree a fast-released multi-vitamin shot. Because these popular water-soluble fertilizers are highly concentrated, mix weak diluted solutions for the first feedings, so as not to "burn" the tender roots. Regardless of the brands used, the first fertilizing should be a weak. Watch and wait, then once a week or once every other week, you can add more. After a couple months or more, then increase the strength to the amount suggested on the package. The seedlings will start to show a response, but you don't want to over-fertilize either. Excessive nitrogen and other nutrients can be washed out of the soil, which causes waste and possible water pollution.

Using granular or slow-release types can be done during the first feedings also. Chelated or specially coated fertilizers can serve the same purpose, which is to reduce the chance of burning the feeder roots. Granular fertilizers can be sprinkled on the soil surface or mulch layer, then thoroughly watered-in. Use a small handful one or twice a month. The water dissolves the salts which filters into the root zone slower because some of the granules won't be fully broken down. So either the water-type or granular approach should work fine.

Basically, fertilizing should be simple since the key is understanding a little bit about fertilizer, then using it in moderation. During the second and three seasons, you can increase the growth rate by more fertilizing, but start with weak applications at first, then build the amounts over time. Planting trees is a long-term program, and the first year is much like having a new-born, take it slow and gradually increase the feedings as establishment increases.

Sunlight and Planting Location

Every plant has varying tolerance to the amount of sun and shade. Too much sun, and a plant may wither or burn. Too little, it may turn yellow and not very grow much. How much light a plant gets is very much a factor of where it is planted.

As general rules, having a house in the center of a circle, the south side is full sun, the north is full shade, the east is early half-day sun, and the west is late half-day sun. What other plants or obstacles are in the area you plant, will effect the amount of light the plant receives.

Fast growing trees like full sun, as much as available. Therefore, you select planting areas that are best suited to the types of trees or plants, in this case full sun for these trees.

Location is important, because once a tree is planted, it quickly becomes difficult to move. Knowing how much light a plant needs, and knowing your yard, you can match the plants requirements for best growth.

Planting

You can plant the Ten as close as six feet apart, or up to ten feet between trees for an effective "green screen" or border. They will grow to about ten to twelve feet wide, and can be easily trimmed or pruned if ever needed. By the time your trees arrive, you will have likely prepared the planting area, removing weeds, maybe tilling the ground, or even putting up animal control fencing (if deer or other animals are a problem).

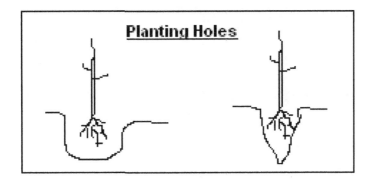

Planting is very easy. Simply, make a hole about 12 inches wide, 12 inches deep, spread the roots out, then re-fill the hole. Do plant the Ameri-Willow deeper than the soil-line to promote additional root formation. Plant them about six inches deeper than the soil-line (the point where roots meet the base of the trunk). This will promote additional rooting along the buried part of the trunk. You don't need to add anything to your soil unless you have heavy clay, rock, or other limiting conditions. If you need to, you can mix in compost, or other soil amendments to break-up the soil, so then the planting hole would need to be a little larger.

After the trees are planted, water them generously. Make sure they are watered and kept moist, especially as the weather gets warmer, namely the summer months. Do put a thick mulch layer around the trees. If you need to, you can provide temporary shading by attaching a piece of cardboard onto a stake placed on the south side of the tree. Blocking the sun for a few hours during the middle of the day can be very beneficial, especially during the first summer. Until Ameri-Willow seedlings are established, they will need a good drink every couple of days or so (depending on your soil conditions and the weather). Just water as needed. A drip system or sprinkler set up works great too.

Spacing

The spacing between the trees is also generalized, depending on the usage. For privacy screens, windbreaks, noise barriers, and other "green walls", you can plant these as close as five or six feet part. Some trees may be better a little further apart, such as planting Sycamore or Kentucky Coffeetree, but Lombardy Poplar might be planted closer together because of its narrow growth habit.

For shade plantings, or as specimens, these can be planted eight to twelve feet apart, or even wider. The Paulownia and oaks are good examples of trees that might be best planted further apart. Consider planting two or more rows. Many people want to combine trees, especially those with different growth rates, so consider planting extra rows. Offset the rows so the space in between will fill in faster. And of course, the more rows you plant, the faster the barrier will fill in and become effective, such as with shelterbelts and windbreaks.

How and where best to plant fast-growing trees? Many of these trees prefer moist areas, and having enough water greatly improves the growth rate. Some of these trees are great shade trees like Weeping Willow, Sycamore, and Poplar. Others are good for borders, privacy screens, or lines, like the Ameri-Willow, Lombardy Poplar, and others. For added beauty, like fall color, Quaking Aspen, maples, and birch are great choices.

To reclaim old pasture or unused land, turning it back into forest, then plant Hybrid Poplars, mulberries, or other hardwoods. Their fast growth will cover the land and the leaves will quickly build up the nutrient and organic matter in the soil. Whether for reforestation, shade, or green-barriers, there are a number of choices to select from!

Plus, there are other trees that grow fast, and have flowers. The broadleafs like - Northern Catalpa, Black and Honey Locusts, the cherries and pears, Tulip Tree, Crape Myrtles, and the Paulownia (Empress Tree). Growth rates do vary considerably, largely due to the actual growing conditions, but planted in fairly good areas, these trees are known to grow quickly.

Although there are evergreens that grow fairly quick, the broad-leafs are much faster growers overall. The Leyland Cypress is one of the most popular and widely spread evergreens planted for fast growth throughout Zones 6 to 10. Once established, these can grow three to four feet a year. but so can the Cryptomeria! Other fast-growing evergreens includes the Hemlock, Western Red Cedar, Coast Redwood in some cases, Eastern White Pine, Scotch Pine, Austrian Pine, the Aleppo and Mondell Pines, Douglas-Fir, and the Norway Spruce. One other fast-growing evergreen to note is the Red-Tip Photinia. Although a tall shrub, this fast-grower is also popularly planted throughout the warmer zones for screens and hedges.

Mulching and Weed Control

Putting a thick layer of mulch around trees and shrubs is always a good idea. The benefits of mulching include soil water conservation, weed control, insulation during the colder months, improved nutrient cycling, as well as keeping the soil temperature around the tree cooler during the summer (which reduces stress on the roots). Use bark or wood chips, straw, lawn clippings, leaves, compost, or other organic materials, at least several inches deep. Some people say that mulch allows bugs, disease, and small critters a safe breeding ground. Yes, this can be true, but you need to monitor this and take corrective actions, just like everything else outdoors, but the benefits of mulching far outweighs the risks.

A thick layer of mulch will aide your trees in growing faster by helping to conserve the soil moisture, helps to reduce the soil from getting too warm (thereby reducing the stress on the roots). Mulch also helps in nutrient cycling, as the mulch decays it improves the soil, and mulch helps to control weeds. Mulching is easy, and typically free.

Mulching is composting, but not as intensively cultured. The mulch naturally breaks down over time, and the nutrients and organic materials filter down into the soil. Some are used by the roots, other materials become part of the "soil" mixture. This is very beneficial, not just from the additional nutrients, but the soil-structure is improved, making air and water cycling better.

If you use your made compost as a mulch layer, that works well too, but good well-seasoned compost is better for mixing into the soil. Raw materials, like leaves or straw, are better to use a mulch.

A thick layer of leaves, lawn clippings, bark, straw, or other materials around your trees offers many benefits. Some people say that mulch allows bugs, disease, and small critters a safe breeding ground. Yes, this can be true, but you need to monitor this and take corrective actions, just like everything else outdoors, but the benefits of mulching far outweighs the risks.

Naturally, controlling weeds by hand-removal, spraying, or repeated cutting, is desirable. Weeds compete for water, sunlight, and nutrients, and often seem to do a better job than our desired plants. Keep them controlled by any means, and those resources will remain available to the tree roots.

Pests, Pathogens, and Animals

Trees and plants have some natural protections against insects and disease, and the best prevention is to keep the plants as healthy as possible. It is also normal and common for insects and disease to attack very healthy trees and plants. Without question, the advent of insects or pathogens, the growth of the trees will be hampered. The greater the attack, the slower the trees or plants will grow, even to the point where they stop growing or die.

The only thing to do is watch your trees. Are there bugs visible or pieces of leaves disappearing? Keeping a close watch will limit a problem, because you take immediate action to spray or remove the damaged or infected parts. Your local garden center can help with identifying pests.

Animals can also have a disastrous impact on trees, especially while they are small. Deer and other herbivores can devastate plants, but domestic animals like goats, horses, and cattle can also strip plants and trees. Fencing, repellents, and other control means may be needed, at least while the trees are small.

Controlling Deer

Privacy screens and windbreaks make great hiding cover for deer. One of the most asked questions has to do with deer. Deer are beautiful animals, and really enjoyable to see... as long as they are not your yard, eating your trees and plants... We too are plagued by these large brown vermin, as well as possums, raccoons, armadillos, skunks, raccoons, rabbits, snakes of various kinds, squirrels, rats, mice, gophers, and even bears.

We rather not apply the 30-30 solution, but rather we try as best we can to live with all of these remarkable creatures. The one exception are the rattlesnakes... we have no tolerance for them! But the question is always, how to keep the deer (in particular) from smashing down the wire fences, sleeping in the tree-beds, and providing them with too many free meals...

There are many people that offer many ideas, and some work, some don't, but deer are not fooled for long. Outside of shooting them or letting them run wild, there can be some sort of control. Deer are most actively in your yard "seasonally", typically when their natural food and water sources are limited. And if deer are having a problem finding food, then chances are good that other animals will view your plants will hungry eyes.

There are deer-resistant trees and shrubs, typically the acidic tasting conifers among other plants, but when they are hungry, they will eat anything, and nibble everything else. Bloodmeal works sometimes, various deer repellents work at other times, and having a dog run around the yard eager to chase anything that moves gets to be annoying after a while.

The best solution is to fence the yard or at least those key and critical plants. The willows and poplars can be very tasty, so having a little fence around them until the trees are big enough to resistant major damage, might be the best plan. Deer are harder than most animals to fence out because the jump so well. A deer can clear an eight foot fence, and they can sometimes jump taller barriers than that. But a fence is the best and primary way to keep them out.

You can cover individual trees or shrubs with netting. The black plastic netting is available at many gardens centers, and its cheap. This might be best when the deer are particularly interested in a few trees, prized specimens, or new plantings.

Many people have luck with repellent materials. A wide variety of these are available in garden centers. Most of them are not appropriate for any type of food-producing tree or plant, so don't... Repellents work one of two ways: by taste or by smell. Taste repellents are usually non-volatile, so last longer. Don't use taste repellents on anything you plan to eat, because you won't like it either. Smell repellents are volatile, so must be reapplied every couple of weeks unless heavy rains prompt you to apply them again. Change repellents every couple of weeks for the best effect.

Which ones work the best is always difficult to say, one may work in one area, but not somewhere else. The idea is that if the deer don't like the way it smells, they re less inclined to devour it. And if it tastes bad, then they tend not to nibble it twice.

Blood meal, which is sold as a soil amendment or fertilizer works, but it stinks. Sprinkle it around the soil and reapply after a rain or every few days. Perfumed soap, like Irish Spring is effective, as are moth-balls. Place some of it near the plants you want protected.

There are sprays made with garlic, rotten meat or eggs, fish emulsion fertilizer, Tabasco sauce and red pepper, etc., all have been successfully used.

Overall, the first defense is the fence around the property. Fencing is typically the most certain way to keep animals out, but they are intrusive, can be expensive, and they do need maintenance or repair at times.

Although electric fencing sounds cruel, they are humane and effective for keeping the animals out. They give a highly unpleasant (but harmless) shock when touched. They are best used as part of an existing fence, and usually to keep animals from climbing over or burrowing under.

With electric fences, its important to control weeds growing under the electric wire. Anything that touches it, will reduce the charge. Electric fences should be left on most of the time, turning them off only when you are working around them.

One of the most innovative approaches to wire electric wire fencing is to train the wild animals using the carrot and a stick thinking. String a single strand of electric fence 2 to 3 feet above the ground. Every 3 feet, tape on a piece of aluminum foil about 3 inches by 3 inches square. Put some peanut butter on each piece of foil. The peanut butter attracts the deer, who then gets a (harmless) shock and they learn to respect the strand of wire.

Keep in mind that deer are intelligent and adaptable. It is more difficult to keep them out of your yard after they have become used to browsing there. The effectiveness of the fence also depends on how hungry they are. Very hungry deer will brave all odds and overcome unusual obstacles to get a free meal. You actually have better luck controlling well-fed deer who are just exploring. Either way, they learn your tricks, so change the repellents and obstacles periodically.

The problem with deer is that they are excellent jumpers. A fence

81

should be at least 8 feet high to keep deer out. And that gets into some real challenges trying to construct it. However, deer are not good at jumping both high and wide. A fence only 4 feet high can keep them out if it is also 4 feet wide. Make a slanted fence by planting 7-foot fence posts at a 45-degree angle, so the top is 4 feet from the ground. The fence should slant away from the plants you are protecting. String woven wire fencing along the fence posts. Make it doubly effective by stringing an electric wire at the top.

The simplest and least expensive deer fence is made of plastic netting, sold at many garden centers. Usually it comes 8 feet high, it can be strung between trees and bushes as well as fence posts. Use this type of fencing for a quick, temporary barrier. Either add this on top of an existing fence, or go with the double-wide fence idea. Since the material is relatively cheap, and very lightweight, you can easily try it.

Use fencing with repellents, and that should keep the deer out... at least most of the time.

Controlling Other Animals

Now many small animals may try to climb a fence, but most are not good jumpers. You can deter possums, skunks, raccoons, and many other climbing animals with a floppy-top fence.

Make the fence of chicken wire or woven wire fencing 4 feet wide. Fence posts should be 2 to 3 feet high. Fasten the wire so the top 18 inches is loose and pull it slightly toward the outside. This makes the "floppy top" that keeps animals from climbing over. As they climb, the top bends back under their weight, keeping them from getting over. A strand of electric wire along the top of a fence will also keep animals from climbing over.

An Apron fences is good for digging animals like rabbits and dogs. They can be kept out with an apron, which is an extension of the fence about 2 feet wide that extends along the ground. Either bury the apron or peg it down tightly to the ground. Burrowing animals will try to dig under the fence at the vertical portion and be deterred by the apron. Small-animal fences can be built with both floppy tops and aprons to deter both climbers and diggers.

And for digging animals, like pocket gophers, armadillos, and mice, that burrow through the soil, bury a portion of the fence. This can work to protect individual trees, small groupings, or lines (like for privacy screens). Use 1-inch mesh or smaller depending on the critter involved. Bury a foot to two feet of fencing around the outside of your planting area. You can protect raised beds by lining the bottoms with chicken wire or hardware cloth before filling them with soil. This simple measure is very effective at avoiding problems with burrowing rodents.

Underground perimeter fences may be more trouble than they're worth, and may not keep gophers out completely, but it is still overall the best way to keep most of the animals out. Gophers can dig several feet deep and make their burrows, and when the fencing is not working, then periodic flooding will get them out (at least for a while).

On HGtv, there was a show about repelling gophers and moles, and they had some interesting ideas. As with deer, there are many methods used to control these pests, including, traps, poisons, flooding the tunnels, fumigants (including using car exhaust piped into the tunnels), and hunting. Each method has some successes, varying costs, as well as other concerns. But on the show, they went with the idea of repelling these pests.

Moles make shallow, typically surface tunnels, as they forage for grubs, bugs, and worms. For the most part, they help aerate the soil and are relatively good. Gophers on the other hand are very bad, since their tunnels are deep and they eat roots of everything we plant. And for both, using granular Castor Oil seems to be very effective. Where you would find it pre-made is anyone's guess, but it is simply a mixture of castor oil, soap (either laundry or dish soap), and corn meal (granulated corn husks or similar starch carrier can be used too). Spread the mixture about 1 pound per 1,000 square feet of ground, water it in, and that is it! You can use lines, put some in key spots, or any type of application you want, its versatile. The granular castor oil method is safe, natural, cheap, and very effective!

And if nothing works, then you might contact your local or state wildlife department to see if they have a better solution.

One note about mosquitoes... They are everywhere, in virtually every climate and habitat. They need water to live, so the drier areas of the country are far less buggy than those that live in the swampy of wetter areas. Here too, there are many types of control methods, each with associated costs and effectiveness. But one of the more unique and very wildlife-friendly ideas to try is Batboxes. There are many species of bats native across the country, and mostly they feed on insects. It was noted on the HGtv show that bats can eat about 6,000 mosquitoes a night! If you will put up bird-house like structures in several trees, that will help provide habitat for bats. Now the holes (or slits) for the bats should be smaller than you would make for most song birds, otherwise the houses will be occupied by birds (not undesirable either). But the idea of bats (and many species of birds) are better at getting rid of mosquitoes and other bugs than we are. Again, its safer, cheaper, and supports wildlife. You can contact the Audubon society, your state wildlife department, and other sources for more information and how to build (or where to buy) bat and bird boxes.

A COUPLE POINTS
TO KEEP IN MIND

The basics of screens and barriers have been examined, followed by the various types of trees to consider when designing such a green wall. And the last section looked at the how-to's of planting, fertilizing, and so on. Among the last questions have to do with how and where to get these trees. As the "big-box" stores and some of the local nurseries might not have many of the desired trees, then mail-order via the internet offers many good sources for planting materials.

The mass production of trees and plants by the growing industry over the past couple of decades have made landscaping afford-able. Still, to do large scale projects, the cost for plant materials can be rather spendy. Therefore, it is better to buy high quality plants from reputable dealers, than to save a few pennies and have to replace them later, or not have the performance you would otherwise get.

Trees & Mail Order

"Spring is just around the corner", as a popular cliche would sug-gest, but planting can happen all year long for many areas of the country. If you can buy your trees locally, do so. The challenge however is that the local "big box" stores, or local nurseries gen-erally will not carry what you want. Hence, the internet and mail order is a big business, and often your only source for plant mater-ials.

Mail order works. It sounds funny to ship trees in the mail, but if its done right, then mail order is the next best thing to being there.

The whole process of shipping and handling can get pretty tech-nical and labor intensive. There is actually quite a lot that goes into it. Timing is important, how its packaged, the materials they're packed with, handling the tree or plants, the shipper, and also how the customer cares for the trees once they arrive, will all influence how well the trees will do. Some trees can be shipped even after they have leafed out, while others just can't handle the shock.

The ideal situation is when the trees are lifted out of the field or greenhouse, then stored in tree coolers. The dormant trees can then be handled extensively (yet gently), shipped, planted, and they will do great once spring rolls around. That step of the pro-cess goes back to the basic concepts of keeping the roots moist and handling the tree so that roots aren't damaged. As long as the roots are intact and kept moist, the plants don't need soil, sunlight, etc. While they are dormant, they can sit for months perfectly fine.

Then when it comes time to packaging and shipping, the same care for the roots is done, as well as protecting the stem for injury. Simply by wrapping them in a material that will maintain cool and moist conditions, the tree still is clueless as to what's happening. Each nursery is different, and uses different materials to hold the moisture, some use shredded newsprint, others use peat moss, and we have a preference for sawdust. Some places use wet newsprint to wrap the plants, others use plastic bags.

Can you fit a 24-inch tree into a 18-inch box? Sort of. Each tree is different, and some will bend, while others break. Ever hear the cliche, "bends like a willow"? In packaging, we do what we have to. Before trees are packaged, they get sorted as to size, and because box size doesn't always match, the choices becomes limited. Trimming the tops of some plants will work, others it deforms the trees. These are factors that have to be juggled, but the care of the seedling is most important.

Once packed, the rest of the trip is in the hands of the shipper. The post office and UPS have gotten a lot better about handling packages, but a well wrapped box will usually survive ok. If a box is tightly packed, then it can't easily compress. If you box a tree in a triangle, it's really hard to crush. Then of course, if its well marked, it helps the box along its journey.

The most fun of mail, is getting a package. When you see that its your trees, carefully open the package. Because its packaged tightly, spent several days at the whims of the shipper, the plants need to be removed. First always, inspect the box. Is it crushed, or is there something positive to say for that physics concept of compression vectors and surface area? Carefully unwrap the trees. Was there breakage or dry roots? Was there a packing slip and/or other information? Water the trees and put them in a cool and shaded area until you are ready to plant. The idea of careful handling and keeping the roots moist, still applies.

Shipping and timing are always good questions, and you can learn more from the website (see below). The Ameri-Willow hybrid is shipped nearly year round, and most commonly via the postal service. You know your area and seasons best, but order early, and take delivery early. Trees can be held in a cool, moist, poorly lit area for some time, but plant as soon as practical.

It is best to take delivery of the trees as early as possible. The trees ship best while dormant, and will site perfectly fine and become acclimated to the new planting conditions. This is particularly important for the northern half of the country that still has wintry or colder weather. Temporarily pot or plant the dormant trees, protecting the roots, then move them to a cool, slightly moist and protected location. This will hold them in a dormant condition, until the ground can be worked. Plant while dormant, which often means while its still chilly.

And although normally shipped while dormant, these trees can also be shipped during the growing season. If shipped during the growing season, they are trimmed them back to look more like sticks, leafless, and they typically resprout within a couple weeks after planting. That reduces the stress on the plant, but they may wilt for a short time during the shipping, they will rebound with zeal. It sounds strange, but the time-tested process produces excellent shipping and planting success.

Once a package arrives, you will want to carefully take your Ameri-Willow trees out of the packaging materials and place them in a bucket of water. It is safe to let the trees stay in water up to a couple weeks, but always best to plant them as soon as practical. Once planted, do place a thick mulch layer around them, and keep watered. It's really a very simple process, with great success.

ABOUT THE AUTHOR AND MORE INFORMATION

Gardening and the growing of plants is really all about soil management. With over 55 years of soil-related experiences, years of schooling and hands-on training, it has led me to share this information about compost making. I hope you found this booklet useful and inspiring.

What we mostly do is grow trees. Trees (and soil) are the crux of our training, with the goal of inspiring people to plant trees. "Even one small seedling can grow into something large and wonderful." With that motto, a number of years ago, we started Empire National Nursery, LLc to promote tree planting.

There are other booklets and guides we offer, revolving around trees and plants, such about Fast-Growing Trees, Berry Shrubs, Tree Planting, and more. For trees and shrubs for the home, farm, or reforestation planting projects, visit us our website:
(http://www.cdr3.com/catalog).

Also learn more about the Ameri-Willow at:
(http://www.cdr3.com/willow).

For Fast-Growing Trees, see:
(http://www.cdr3.com/growers).

Get the Book

We have a growing library of eBooks on Amazon Kindle. Most are about trees, an associate of non-tree subjects authors some. You found this book, but check out the others. Go to Amazon.com, and search the Kindle Books link for William A. Jack (author). Or, you can enter the ASIN number of the book.

Consider these titles:

Compost 101: Simple How-to Make and Recycle Your Organic Wastes
By William A. Jack
ASIN: B07FY7JDTZ

How to Plant and Grow the Paw Paw Tree
By William A. Jack
ASIN: B07GDKX2ZC

...

How-to Plant and Grow the Black Aronia Berry
By William A. Jack
ASIN: B07GBNVDV6

Easy How-to Plant and Grow Blueberries
By William A. Jack
ASIN: B07GZTC9S5

Easy How-to Plant and Grow the Ameri-Willow Tree: For fast growing Privacy Screens and Windbreaks
By William A. Jack
ASIN: B07H5SCK75

How-to Plant and Grow Mulberry Trees

By William A. Jack
ASIN: B07GC7331Q

How-to Plant and Grow Colorado Blue Spruce Trees
By William A. Jack
ASIN: B07HHHF6YS

Simple How-to Plant and Grow Quaking Aspen Trees
By William A. Jack
ASIN: B07H4TRS1B

Easy How-to Plant and Grow European White Birch Trees
By William A. Jack
ASIN: B07H42BJBV

Simple How-to Plant and Grow Horsechestnut, Ohio Buckeye, and Red Buckeye Trees: 3 Trees for Shade in the Landscape
By William A. Jack
ASIN: B07H3BHWCH

The Empire of Trees: The ListBot Articles of Trees for Home Garden Landscaping and Reforestation Projects
By William A. Jack
ASIN: B07KPYYS4D

The Empire of Seeds: The ListBot Articles of Seeds for Home Garden Landscaping
By: William A. Jack
ASIN: B07KSGLZ4X

Simple How-to Plant and Grow Blackberries
By: William A. Jack
ASIN: B07MJC38TS

And, those written by Thomas Logwood, includes:

A Walk in the Sub-Alpine Meadows: A Look at the Tuolumne Meadows Ecosystem
ASIN: B07HM928TH
By T. H. Logwood

Collecting Old Stock Certificates: A Look at the Past
ASIN: B07HNX1FGK
By T. H. Logwood

The End of American Freedom: Free Speech Can Die in the 2020 Election
By T. H. Logwood
ASIN: B07MSJ4QD7

The U.S.S. La Porte (APA 151), The Pearl of the Pacific
By T. H. Logwood
ASIN: B07L6JXRB9

Printed in Great Britain
by Amazon

41996042R00057